1997
.50

Blizman
P9-CFN-729
33 September Ln.
Beacon Falls, CT 06403

Sandy Dennis
A Personal Memoir

Sandy Dennis
A Personal Memoir

Co-edited by Louise Ladd and Doug Taylor
Foreword by Joanne Woodward

PAPIER-MACHE PRESS
WATSONVILLE, CA

Copyright © 1997 by the Estate of Sandra Dale Dennis. Printed in Singapore. All rights reserved including the right to reproduce this book or portions thereof in any form. For information contact Papier-Mache Press, 135 Aviation Way, #14, Wat-sonville, CA 95076.

01 00 99 98 97   5 4 3 2 1

ISBN: 1-57601-001-5 Hardcover

Cover and interior design by Leslie Austin
Text composition by Leslie Austin
Cover photograph: *People Weekly* © 1989 Marianne Barcellona
Co-edited by Louise Ladd and Doug Taylor
Proofreading by Erin Lebacqz and Shirley Coe

Photo credits:
childhood photographs, courtesy of Frank Dennis; page xii courtesy of Walton C. Ferris Sr.; page xiv from the private collection of Chandler Davis; page xix courtesy of St. Vincent's Medical Center; page 4 from UPI/Corbis-Bettmann Archive; pages 20, 62, 66, and 70 from *People Weekly* © 1989 Marianne Barcellona; page 48 courtesy of Westport Country Playhouse; and page 54 from UPI/Corbis-Bettmann.

Library of Congress Cataloging-in-Publication Data
Dennis, Sandy.
      Sandy Dennis: a personal memoir.
         p. cm.
      ISBN 1-57601-001-5 (cloth: alk. paper)
       1. Dennis, Sandy. 2. Actors—United States—Biography. I. Title.
PN2287.D386A3   1996
791.43'028'092—dc20
[B]   96-30607
                                        CIP

The Estate of Sandy Dennis and the editors wish to thank our agent, Mary Jack Wald.

Had it not been for her continued devotion to Sandy's writing talent this book would not have been published.

★ ★ ★ ★ ★

Contents

$\mathcal{T}$hose of you who knew Sandy Dennis primarily as an actress, as I did, may share my amazement and delight in discovering that she also had a highly original, quite exceptional talent as a writer. Her work appears effortless, and I found a sense of freedom I hadn't expected, as well as the true eye and ear and imagination of a writer, expressed in what I would call an almost Emily Dickensonian sensibility.

I opened *Sandy Dennis: A Personal Memoir,* expecting the usual Hollywood memoir, and from the first sentence of the first chapter I found myself completely absorbed—drawn in by the air of mystery created— to a place and time so alluring that I was compelled to read on. I was swept along, flowing back and forth in time, fascinated by the search and growth of the child, who became the child that still lived within the adult.

We become privy to glimpses of Sandy, child and adult, through her extraordinary eye for details. She had an ability to really *see* what was going on around her, to recall memories, to recapture images with a preciseness and economy of words that vividly recreate those moments for the reader.

Sandy was almost as well known for her love of cats as she was for her many memorable films and plays. I've always thought her dedication to otherwise unwanted cats was nice, as I like cats too (although I've never had as many, perhaps three or four or five at a time). Reading this book, I discovered Sandy wasn't just someone who had a lot of cats; this was a person who had relationships with four-footed creatures who just happened to be cats. But they could very well have been children, or friends, or anyone with whom she had close personal ties. Each one was a unique individual to her, and thus becomes so to the reader.

Funny situations often arise when you have animals in the house, and Sandy writes of them with an elegant and dainty sense of humor. Her depictions are so beautifully crafted one can't help but chuckle in sympathy as she copes with both the mundane and the unexpected results of life in such a household.

While writing this book, Sandy had already been diagnosed with the cancer that would end her life at the age of fifty-four. I admire her courage and singular approach to handling her illness. When I finished reading her stories I felt a true sadness, not only for her death, but for the loss of her unique voice and talent. What a tragedy that she wasn't able to continue writing for many more years to come.

—Joanne Woodward

$\mathcal{I}$ stood in Sandy Dennis's empty house, studying a framed photograph of a dog, my duties as administrator of her estate forgotten. The feeling that I knew this animal was strong. "It's Brown Dog," I heard myself say as my mind rushed back through the years to Philadelphia's Playhouse-in-the-Park.

It was 1972. Sandy and my then wife, Barbara Baxley, longtime friends, were starring in a summer tour of Paul Zindel's *And Miss Reardon Drinks a Little*. A small brown stray had taken refuge near the theater and Sandy began to feed her. When I arrived for the closing night performance, Sandy announced she was adopting the dog and asked if I would drive them back to Westport, Connecticut. This meant a detour for her, as the rest of the company would be taking a bus directly to the next theater.

As I was going to nearby Weston, I readily agreed. I would have acquiesced no matter what my destination, for I had developed a deep

affection and respect for Sandy. We talked for most of the trip, further cementing our friendship. Brown Dog, as she was later named, curled at her mistress's feet and slept for the entire journey, confident that she had found someone to care for her for the rest of her days.

Sandy Dennis achieved stardom early in her career. Cast as a charming, disoriented social worker in Herb Gardner's *A Thousand Clowns* opposite Jason Robards, she won the Tony Award for Best Supporting Actress. She triumphed again the following season, winning a second Tony as Best Actress for her performance in Muriel Resnick's *Any Wednesday* opposite Gene Hackman. Then director Mike Nichols asked her to be in his film version of *Who's Afraid of Virginia Woolf?* with Elizabeth Taylor, Richard Burton, and George Segal—earning Sandy the coveted Oscar for Best Supporting Actress. As her fame soared, she also became well-known as a lover of cats. Few knew, however, that she had an equal affection for dogs and people, taking many a human stray needing friendship under her motherly wing, and frequently into her home.

I first met Sandy on a Sunday afternoon in Barbara's East Thirty-fourth Street apartment. Sandy was dropping by to borrow a dress to wear at a prerehearsal gathering for her first major Broadway role. Barbara had played Sandy's mother on the national tour of William Inge's *The Dark at the Top of the Stairs*, and their mother-daughter relationship had spilled over into their everyday lives. They originally met at a summer theater in Florida during rehearsals for Inge's *Bus Stop*. Sandy tried out for the role of Alma, claiming she had played the part before. Barbara, a savvy Broadway veteran, knew two minutes into rehearsals that Sandy was inexperienced and had not been in *Bus Stop*. However, it was clear this fresh young talent was perfect for Alma, so Barbara surreptitiously guided Sandy's movements with whispered instructions and secret signals. Both took great satisfaction in knowing the director never caught on.

Barbara opened the apartment door, and I caught my first glimpse of Sandy Dennis. She was casually dressed in clothes that did little, if anything, to enhance her natural attractiveness. She wore no makeup, and apparently gave her hair passing attention at best. She held up the two dresses Barbara had laid out, one a slender form-fitting, strapless black wool, the other a two-piece almond outfit with a pleated skirt. Without a word, she went to change in the bedroom.

Moments later, a startlingly beautiful creature in black emerged, filling the room with a stunning sexuality. She crossed to the full-length mirror and began to giggle as she angled her body this way and that, creating curves and poses that would have shamed Marilyn Monroe.

Barbara and I expressed our enthusiastic approval. Sandy went back to the bedroom and returned in the almond outfit, looking every bit the lovely English schoolgirl on her way to tea with a duchess. Ignoring our opinion, she chose the more sedate outfit, quietly gathered her items, and said her good-byes. Content with her selection and the aura she

emanated, Sandy Dennis closed the door behind her and walked out of our Sunday afternoon toward stardom.

It was strange being in the empty house that Sandy had once filled with life and living. During my visits, Sandy, her mother Yvonne, and I had gathered in the kitchen. Ours was a kitchen friendship—warm and loving, with a strong sense of camaraderie.

Now as I wandered the rooms I could feel Sandy's presence. I climbed the wide, curving staircase—a perfect setting for a film about the old South—and made my way to Sandy's office. There were books everywhere. She was an avid reader and a collector, and the house was filled with books, ten thousand in all. Two metal file cabinets stood in one corner of the office. The bottom drawer of one held only a few items, mostly scraps of paper and some manila folders that looked vaguely familiar. Inside one folder I found handwritten sheets of yellow, legal-sized notepaper. It was a chapter of Sandy's manuscript.

I'm not certain when she first mentioned she was writing a book. I do recall we were sitting in her kitchen, cats perched here and there, dogs sprawled at our feet, when she said, "I've been writing."

She was an excellent photographer, and I asked if she meant captions to go with the photos I'd been urging her to publish. "No, it's a book," she replied.

She had only completed two chapters but agreed to let me take them home. I was captivated by her unique voice and offered to send her work to a literary agent. Sandy was pleased but felt she should finish a few more chapters first.

A month later, I inquired about the book's progress and learned of her snail-paced method of creating. Slowly writing and rewriting the chapters by hand, she then turned them over to a friend to type. But the friend was away at the moment, so there were no new chapters. Having been a playwright for many years and used to working under deadlines, I questioned the wisdom of waiting, but Sandy's reply, as always, was simple and direct: "If I didn't want to wait for her, I wouldn't."

Now I stood in her office holding a chapter I hadn't seen. Due to the complications of Sandy's illness and my own involvements, I had not read beyond the first two chapters. I searched deeper in the cabinet drawers and found the completed manuscript.

It was a balmy spring day. I sat outside on a wrought iron bench and began to read. Once again I was transported into the special moments in Sandy's life: her childhood, her adulthood, her loves and joys, her laughter, her pain and courage facing death. When I closed the cover on the final chapter, I stared across the garden, awash with yellow daffodils, into the woods beyond. After thirty years of friendship, of countless intimate and casual conversations, of facing numerous crises together, and seeing almost every one of her performances, I had only now touched the essence that was Sandy Dennis.

At home, I gave the manuscript to Louise Ladd, a professional writer and editor, who was equally taken by Sandy's prose. Louise's agent, Mary Jack Wald, agreed to read it and her response was immediate and glowing. She asked us to prepare the manuscript for submission to publishers. As principal editor, Louise immediately became the champion of Sandy's creative legacy, avoiding any changes that might distort intentions or meanings. And now, five years later, the book will be available to the public on Sandy's sixtieth birthday, April 27, 1997.

Sandy's ovarian cancer was diagnosed in 1989, but over the next three years she continued to work whenever possible. She especially enjoyed teaching acting at HB Studios in New York. She'd studied with Herbert Berghof, whom she adored, and found the classes she taught for him and Uta Hagen very rewarding.

After Sandy underwent her third and final operation, I took to visiting with her two or three afternoons a week, when she was alone. I treasured these quiet moments with her. Although her illness must have been emotionally shattering, she was usually able to handle it with wry humor and an earthy, matter-of-fact acceptance. Mostly we spoke of other things—old friends, old loves, the theater, teaching, our mutual yesterdays.

Sandy never hesitated to tell a good story on herself, particularly those with a humorous touch of irony. One afternoon we were discuss ing teaching, and Sandy suddenly sat up in bed and told me about the time a student's mother, Liv Ullmann, the Swedish actress, observed one of her classes. As luck (or fate) would have it, two students were presenting a scene from *A Doll's House,* by Ibsen, a play Ms. Ullmann surely knew well.

"They didn't have the scene at all," Sandy confessed. "So I started to work with them, and the more I directed them the worse the scene became. And all the while, Liv just sat there, slumped in her chair, staring at the actors. It was excruciating, it was dreadful," she laughed. I laughed with her, for it was truly a teacher's ultimate nightmare.

Sandy Dennis was one of the most unpretentious people I've met. I never thought of her as being a star, for in all the years I knew her she never once behaved like one. I recall asking if she missed acting. "Not a bit," she promptly replied. "I miss *teaching* acting though, and not being able to clean my house and care for the animals."

One of our editorial tasks was locating pictures of Sandy offstage. There were amazingly few pictures of Sandy in her files, or anywhere in her house. However, in her mother's room, in the back of an otherwise empty drawer, I discovered a small wrought iron-framed photo of a teenager. I stared at it, fascinated by the girl with hair flowing to her shoulders. She appeared quiet, withdrawn, as though she didn't want to attract attention. The handwriting on the back confirmed that it was taken for Sandy's high school graduation. I also found two tiny framed portraits showing Sandy at a younger age, possibly eight or nine, embracing a cat. One image was somber; the other revealed a joyous little girl, seemingly pleased with herself, her life, and her cat.

Later I discovered a picture of Sandy surrounded by women in clown costumes, taken in 1987 at St. Vincent's Health Center, a hospital in Bridgeport, Connecticut. A friend of mine, Pat Plumb, chaired that year's Employee's Giving Campaign, a fund to help offset health costs for the poor. She needed someone special to kick off the campaign. Sandy, still recovering from her first cancer operation (performed at another hospital), agreed to lend her support.

At the celebration, Sandy gave herself fully to the staff, greeting each employee with her warm midwestern exuberance. She made them feel as if they were talking with a friend, not a famous actress. Her innate humanness was especially apparent during those moments of spontaneity, and they adored her.

At one point the ladies dressed as clowns surrounded her and the photographer clicked off a shot. Now I stood in Sandy's kitchen, holding the picture as daylight vanished into evening. Time to go. I slipped the photo into my bag and left, taking with me the memory of the day Sandy gave so much of herself with such love.

—Doug Taylor

World, World, I cannot get thee close enough!

—Edna St. Vincent Millay

Sandy Dennis
A Personal Memoir

Three Pennies

$\mathcal{I}$ walked, that hot summer afternoon, past the Fises' croquet lawn and cut across the empty street. Waves of heat lifted from the tarred road, burning my bare young feet. I stepped up onto the curb and into the cool grass. Time hung endless and full that afternoon as I made my way up the sidewalk and entered the tiny neighborhood store. A small paper-white house. One room had been made into a convenience store. Inside the screen door I stood on the soft wood floor. A long wooden counter seemed to stretch endlessly the length of the room. I had come for jawbreakers. I could have three, perhaps four, as Blond Dolly often gave extras. I was patient with anticipation. In time someone would come, and I would choose and go out into the day to sit on the back stairs of our house on that corner lot and suck on my jawbreakers.

How long did I wait in that empty store, pennies in my hand? I did not know time then. I dreamed and waited. I shifted and counted the tiny Xes that ran across the front of my smocked dress. I walked the length of the counter to the door at the back of the store. It was open and led downstairs to the basement. I started down the stairs, hands on the wooden railing. Halfway down, I saw hanging from the ceiling a person, a grown, sexless person. I recognized death but without compassion or fear. It was cooler now, halfway into the basement. Many years later in Moscow, as I descended the stairs to gaze at Lenin resting waxy in his glass coffin, the coolness started to invade my senses and I remembered that long ago summer afternoon. I remembered like a painting one could walk into and stay for a time and then return to one's own life.

Everything was very still that afternoon. I stood halfway down those stairs, holding onto the wooden railing. I turned and walked back up the stairs and stood at the counter in front of the glass jars filled with jawbreakers. I could take what I wanted. I knew there was no one in that store. I had no sense of violence. I slipped the three pennies from my hand onto the counter, stood on my tiptoes and lifted the tin lid of the slanted glass jar, chose three black jawbreakers, and walked past the screen door that closed behind me with a gust of sealed air. I walked out into the white hot summer afternoon, retracing my steps, the jawbreakers melting, sticky in my hands. I put one into my mouth, stuck it in the side of my cheek, and waited for the sweet licorice taste to flood my mouth.

I must have been three that summer, the summer I knew it was wrong to take something. It was the first occasion I remember of a moral decision made entirely on my own. The color and heat of that day, the taste of licorice, the sidewalks ribboning home. The empty lot on the corner, tall with weeds and hollyhock. The smocked dress I wore. Sticky hands.

The silence of that thousand-year-old endless afternoon remains a mystery without attached emotion.

Almost half a century later I remain primarily an observer. I carry images stored in dusty places, not properly cataloged, hidden in corners, with a shaft of light from the window filled with dust and cat hairs. The color of a lamp shade in a strange window, the smell of a brick wall, can tumble these images into restored moments, like slides projected on a screen.

I rarely recall emotions. I recall images. Bowls of tulips drooping in the hotel suite in London, while a rarely seen snowstorm raged outside. The jagged body movement of a lover in the twilight of my kitchen, before an unprecedented attack of physical violence. The grey-blue mist of smoke rising from the fall bonfires in the graveyard high above Saint Paul.

Circle of Soft Light

*T*oday is the first day of spring. The official first day. It is late afternoon and the wind is unrelenting. The tall evergreen outside the window where I write whips against the house like ropes, and I am thrown into such anguish. I fear everything. Foolish, foolish very real fear. This morning for an hour, unexpected snow fell, thick quick flakes covering the trees and ground. Within minutes it disappeared. The sun came and went. Now this wind digs an empty space.

The cats have crawled into the back of the bookcase and pushed books all over the floor. Someone has chewed the corner off *Seeing with the Mind's Eye: The History, Techniques, and Uses of Visualization*. It is impossible to place blame. The resident group of cats currently living in these upstairs rooms is five, but can swell to a dozen or more during the day.

I strongly suspect Paula Carlene of the book damage. A tortoise cat with a face like a checkerboard, intelligent placid eyes, and a perfect tiny head placed on one of the largest fat cat bodies I have ever seen, she sleeps now, barely visible on my down comforter. Awake, she fancies paperback books. She eats them, not in secret but openly, with great chomping pleasure. I found her eleven years ago at the tail end of a hurricane, outside my hotel room in Florida, so tiny then I could almost hold her in one hand, visions of millions of meals dancing in her head. I ordered breakfast and she ate it—scrambled eggs, buttered whole wheat toast, bacon, cream—stopping only at juice and coffee.

I spent the morning trying to find out if she belonged to someone. It seems I have spent a major part of my life clutching one cat or another, searching for a bereaved owner. All over the world, cats in my arms are met by a blank expression reserved for a madwoman. Have I ever found a grateful owner? I can't remember one. That particular wet morning no one spoke English, or perhaps no one wanted to, and certainly no one recognized this tiny kitten. So that afternoon I moved to the apartment that had been prepared for me with a new, unclaimed cat. I lived in that apartment complex for ten weeks, surrounded by young singles. I was able, without too much effort, to acquire eight cats in those ten weeks.

Days after settling in, along came a momma cat with two outrageously beautiful kittens, tiny fine long-haired kittens, curly tufts of wispy fur peeking from their ears. I wondered how she had done it, this thin, ordinary, spotted black-and-white cat, and how inordinately proud she seemed. I caught them with a beach towel, one after the other. I struck quickly from the rear, soon after I had placed a large plate of food on the grass.

Once in the apartment, the kittens discovered the drapes. Their tiny feet rarely hit the floor. They hung suspended, swinging with pleasure, while their mother refused to come out from under the bed. The kittens occasionally joined her there for meals. Momma cat took all of hers under the bed until I hauled her out, howling, to be spayed.

On her return, she called a halt to the free meals but decided on a routine of cleanliness that bordered on madness. No one was spared; even Paula Carlene was pinned to the floor. Every inch was covered. Momma cat pursued them without mercy. They all took to the drapes, Paula's ever-increasing bulk causing large gaps in the fragile beige fabric. They were to be my second pair of floor-to-ceiling drapes replaced at some expense on my exit from a rented home.

Today, eleven years later, Momma cat lies on a box of old photos, her legs tucked under her against the wind, watching me as I sit writing. She's now a round gentle cat, simply called Momma. One of her daughters lives in my mother's room, an only cat except for nights when two orange toms are allowed in to sleep. She reigns queen. My mother claims she is a miniature cat and tells this to people who believe her, for she believes it herself. She is small, it is true, never having grown, in my opinion, either in body or mind. My mother disagrees, and she should know, for they live incestuously in the dark green room at the top of the stairs, watching television and smoking cigarettes. If I dare to go in, she rushes wildly about on short little legs while continually emitting a high-pitched squeak.

Once, a few years ago, my mother went on vacation, and I brought Momma down from the green room. It seemed to me she rather enjoyed being included. Perhaps I read the signs wrong, for she had a kind of fit and fell off the kitchen table and had to be rushed to the vet. I returned her to the green room and, once restored, she returned to herself.

My Florida cat family grew by four more one afternoon when I returned home to find a cardboard box filled with kittens. Earlier that day I had made what I considered an impassioned, eloquent plea for neutering and spaying on a local TV interview show. Someone was watching. I had positive proof: four kittens and a note that read, "Put your money where your mouth is."

That very evening, as I emptied my growing amount of trash, I found a half-grown cat tied securely in a heavy nylon laundry bag and deposited in the dumpster. He was the most magnificent of acquisitions, a pale, pale, creamy-orange half-Siamese, lovely rough, tough boy cat.

It is growing dark now, and I go downstairs to the kitchen. Everywhere cats are gathering for evening treats, sitting on counters, asleep in baskets, warming themselves under lamps. A great mound of cats curl together on the long kitchen table. Mary Frances is asleep in a big blue-and-white mixing bowl. Bonnie has torn up the front page of the *New York Times* and lies content in a paper nest.

I sit alone with a glass of wine in this large white kitchen filled with things I have collected, listening to the gentle crunching of some forty cats eating tiny multishaped bits of dry food. From the chair facing the window I can see the perfect crack from top to bottom in the yellow glass shade of my lamp, broken in a failed flying leap from the top of the refrigerator to the yellow table. I must always remember that these cats care not at all for my things—so many broken things over the years—vases, plates, cups, lamps. The corners of my soft pine chests are shredded, the rungs of chairs like whittled sticks, and tables bear long scars of sliding cats.

I had a lovely, funny, fat cat called Octavia who used to back up and pee into the telephone jacks, causing a complete shutdown and labored explanations to the phone company. Last year the condenser in the refrigerator burned up. The repairman discovered abnormal amounts of cat hair which had collected and caught fire. Exclamations of horror and surprise seemed pointless. The man was standing in a kitchen filled with some thirty very interested cats and they weren't bald.

I have a long narrow table in the kitchen, painted years ago in bright yellow enamel. It has been with me a long time and bears many scars. It now sits under the window and is never empty. The cats watch the world through this window and I watch with them. In this almost darkness, the yellow glass lamp creates a circle of soft light, and I can forget for a second all the fears I carry. In this early darkness there is a kind of momentary peace.

My romantic image of myself surrounded by my cats, my possessions, and soft light is shattered by the arrival in the garage of a very large bird. A group of five cats and Lady, my golden retriever, are gathered around this big bird that is wedged between the trash can and the wall. I start to scream at the top of my lungs at all of them. I do this in any emergency concerning birds, moles, chipmunks, squirrels, snakes, rabbits, large bugs, or other unrecognizable creatures carried by mouth, cornered, or otherwise betrayed. I use vile words and wave my arms. This display is usually met with unblinking dignity, and what I think might be a kind of embarrassment for my behavior. I continue all flapping movements and change my tone to a high-pitched shriek. I have now gained the attention of about twelve other cats, who come gliding out from the open kitchen door on big cat feet. Frankly, I think there is a deep desire to see me in this vulnerable and uncontrolled situation.

Finally I gather all my courage, pick up this very big bird, place it in a cat box, and rush to the den, followed by a now thoroughly interested group of about two dozen cats. After a cigarette and another glass of wine I am able to begin my examination of this large bird, which consists of one quick look in the box. The bird's eyes are open. This gives me confidence. I manage to place a saucer of water and some bread crumbs in the box. A third glass of wine, more confidence. This is a brown bird with almost no wings and a long tail. I consider the possibility of a female pheasant. My mother, who has been alerted by the noise, suggests a bald eagle. I suggest dinner and bed. The morning will bring a dead bird or a live bird. Years of birds in boxes overnight have taught me this.

Unreserved Love

As I struggle out of sleep I start to let go of the dream. I am running across a field and a horse, a deep red-brown horse, is running after me, pulling at my hair with his teeth. I am not frightened, but amused and surprised. I know I am on my way to gather up bathing suits for a swim—but who is with me? There are people. I know them. And there is water and it is inviting. But only the horse stays, with his great white teeth, and the turning of my head in surprise, and a summer day.

And so I wake now. I'm past fifty and alone in this bed, in this room I have picked for this season and for this time, when nothing gives comfort. I wake between three and four every morning, surrounded by cats. I disturb no one but myself. These are my favorite hours, this dark before light. It comes earlier now, in March. The light streaks my window like layers of pale colored sand. I will have to learn not to regret the coming of the dawn. It is not the light I mind, but the loss of this secret time where things are still familiar and without edge.

When I was young I had a radio, a cream-colored plastic radio, all rounded, no sharp edges. In the night when I woke to the silence I would turn it on and as it warmed up, the glow from the filament inside the tiny bulb would leak from the brown cardboard back and I would move through the night, half sleeping and half waking, lulled with the sound of soft senseless voices and a tiny glow of orange in that small first bedroom. The first room I did not have to share. My own room at the back of that last house in Nebraska.

In 1941, the summer after I turned four, we moved from the house of my first concrete memories. The day we left was warm and sunny. My best friend stood teetering on the curb in a yellow summer sunsuit that buttoned to the bottom, a row of white buttons marching all around his middle. We waved that day until we lost sight of one another.

With the new house came a dog we called Skippy, a kind of wire-haired, black-and-white dog, with a tail that curled tight in the shape of a snail. He was, and would remain always throughout his full life, exclusively my mother's.

He was a stray who had been living in the garage of the empty house. For the summer months he remained there, unapproachable. He would eat the food brought to him by my mother. We could not touch him.

During the day he would leave the garage to sit in the field behind our house, only his head visible above the tall weeds. And then one day, at the time when the evenings were starting to become cold and leaves were collecting in the basement window wells, an uncle came for a visit. He held the door open for the dog who had followed him up the front steps and onto the porch, giving the perfect imitation of a well-adjusted family dog. Skippy entered that small midwestern living room and casually crawled under the tall windup Victrola. And from this spot in our house he would follow my mother with his eyes. I, too, crawled under the Victrola, and was bitten. I was more surprised than hurt. Mother took his side, as she was to do for the next eighteen years of his life. He would move with us to different towns, to live in strange rooms, carrying with him a continuing vendetta against the human race, in particular paper boys and meter readers. What secret fear, what images lived in his

dog brain that drove him to such unacceptable social behavior and seemed to fill him with such unimaginable pleasure?

He lived secure in the passionate and unreserved love of my mother. There was the Fourth of July when we went to Crystal Lake. What long, endless days those were. Holidays orchestrated by grown-ups. Hampers filled with food: fried chicken, potato salad, deviled eggs, Kool-Aid for the children, and that secret odd drink that made adults behave so differently. Mother wore a bandanna wound around her head and tied in the front with a kind of small twist in the middle of her forehead, slacks with pleats, and a blouse tied at the waist. We had a stack of firecrackers bought from Big Jim Oder, who sat in an improvised stand, calm among boxes scattered and stacked. He would sit in that hot July sun, a rumored three hundred pounds, wiping away torrents of perspiration with a giant blue-and-white handkerchief.

That day, that particular day, sometime in the late afternoon before dark, before the fireworks started to fill the sky above the lake, someone slightly drunk declared that all dogs could swim; a dog thrown into the water would surface and swim. Against my mother's protestations, Skippy was carried to the end of the wooden dock that stretched out into Crystal Lake and dropped into the water. It was that time of evening, when everyone was a little drunk and happy and believed indeed in the surfacing of this black-and-white dog, who would soon swim to shore and shake himself and run around excitedly. Skippy refused the scenario and remained submerged deep in the lake. My mother joined him. Terrified of water, unable to swim, she jumped in feet first, holding her nose. It seems then in my memory that everyone jumped.

Old age failed to mellow the dog. He tolerated the many other animals that came and went in our lives, as he was to eventually tolerate the first two grandchildren who pulled and plagued him. Stoic, he would sit under the kitchen table, covered with baby fingers. I think he had struck some kind of bargain with my mother—she who had taught him to sing, sit up, roll over, speak, shake hands; she who had saved him from the murky depths of Crystal Lake. He would not bite her grandchildren, sensing the probability that her love for him far outdistanced her love for those two little girls. He could afford to be grand.

He had been taught by my Aunt Adrienne to walk through the house carefully on that foot of exposed wood between the wall and the carpet. He would tap his way to the kitchen without a glance at that 9x15 Sears rug scattered with large full-blown flowers in varying shades of purple and rose. In the living room, the front door opened directly onto wall-to-wall carpeting. He would solve the problem by walking around the edge, never directly across. That large pieces of furniture lined the wall perplexed him not at all. He hugged them, and straightened up with a kind of familiarity as he approached the dining room, where the old rose carpet provided him with a familiar foot of wood.

Never allowed on any piece of furniture in our presence, he always slept curled on the sofa in the front room when we left the house. For years, he never failed to hear the car arrive, or our footsteps on the front porch. Before we reached the door, the long march had begun. We wouldn't find him on the sofa, but stretched out under the yellow Formica table in the kitchen, pretending to wake from a long guiltless sleep.

As he grew older, and increasingly deaf, we would return home to find him sleeping in the middle of the sofa, peacefully dreaming, I've always suspected, of fleeing paper boys on bicycles and mauled grand-children. Neither he nor my mother ever acknowledged this breach of etiquette. He would wake and remove himself from the sofa with dignity, and make slowly for the familiar spot under the kitchen table. When the time came and he could no longer see or hear and had to be carried down the steps to the backyard, when chasing and biting and barking and rolling in anything that smelled bad had become distant memories, my brother took him to be put to sleep and my mother took to her bed.

Somewhere there is a picture of me standing with my Aunt Adrienne. I am dressed in a favorite maroon coat with a herringbone pattern and a darker maroon velvet collar. A hat trimmed in velvet is tied under my chin, and Skippy is sitting on the cement stoop. He was the first animal I remember. He was not mine.

Twenty-Seven Acres of Woods

Twenty-two years ago I found a house to rent on twenty-seven acres of woods. For fourteen years I lived in that house, fourteen years of cats and dogs and visiting nieces. A man I lived with for eleven years left that house. He had found someone else, and I remained there, learning to live alone with increasing pleasure.

A bed of lilies of the valley pushed its way every year closer to the house, and sometimes the fragrance would fill the green dining room and I would escape back to childhood, when I slept in a room with the walls covered in pink-and-blue plaid wallpaper, the woodwork like a ribbon of pale blue satin. And outside my window, outside the pink café curtains I had made from sheets, copied from a picture in *Seventeen* magazine, there was another bed of those small perfect slender stalks. The scent would sometimes wake me on those mornings when everything was possible.

Mary came to the rented house to stay with me; Mary who had first come to dress me in the theater and with whom I spent the next fifteen years of my life. She was not only my housekeeper, but my hook on the world. When she left, parts of me became scattered. I've never found them, never collected the bits and pieces, for she always brought them to me on the palms of her long-fingered hands. Only a few years older than I am now, how did she know so much? She taught me to laugh at myself, taught me patience and the gift to keep certain things secret. I think she is the one person I love without reservation, and I miss her every day.

We moved, Mary and I, after fourteen years to a second house on the same land, this large house I live in now, where I watch the trees disappear, for they have begun to bring the woods down. I knew the time would come, for the land around me had been sold. But I was, as always (for it is a major character flaw), unprepared for the loss and certainly not prepared for the extent of the damage. These trees are brought so easily to the ground by a machine that seems simply to drive into them and they come crashing down like tiny sticks. Soon after they are leveled, a second machine comes along and eats the smaller downed trees and spits them into chips. Miniature mountains of chips are forming everywhere. The very big trees, too big to eat, are carried away quickly on a truck as long as a railway car.

We moved cats, dogs, furniture, some five thousand books, and our lives to this house. Three cats remained in the old house. Change was not in their stars. Two, who were firmly ensconced high in the basement ceiling, refused all coaxing, crying, or pleading. Little Boy had been born in my New York apartment, and his first move to the country had resulted in a three-month living arrangement in the basement pipes. Now a second move seemed out of the question. Carrington, his companion in the maze of the basement ceiling, had been born in the very house she now refused to vacate. Delivered in an upstairs bedroom to a completely surprised and unprepared mother, she—an only child—had plopped out, walked around wobbly, blind and screaming. I had never witnessed such a phenomenon. The thought occurred to me that something unusual had taken place in cat births. What proved to be unusual was that such a large and forward-seeming baby could grow into such a large and backward girl. Her mother, after overcoming her disbelief that such a strange apparition could have found its way into the bedroom, took herself to the highest bookshelf.

Now grown up and witless, perhaps from lack of maternal care—though I felt I had done my part and more—Carrington and Little Boy joined forces and removed themselves to the basement rafters. For days before the new tenant was due, I walked back and forth between the two houses carrying plates of food. I pleaded, I coaxed, I cursed. Two sets of gold eyes stared down at me without pity. In the end I fell back on brute force and pulled them screaming, howling, and hissing to the new house, where they both promptly behaved as if I had made a ridiculous amount of fuss over nothing. After all, they had intended to eventually walk over sometime and see the new place.

Little Boy became one of the kitchen cats, a group so named because they rarely, and some of them never, leave the kitchen and pantry area. This kitchen community is largely based on food, warmth, and companionship, mainly my mother's food, warmth, and companionship. She spends a great many of her waking hours sitting in a big chair at the kitchen table. Occasionally she has been known to eat and is found to be generous—or if not generous, too tired to fight for her food—unlike myself, who has been known to wrestle a cat to the floor for a tuna sandwich.

The last holdout in the old house was a small black cat, called Beasty, who had disappeared at the first sign of impending change. She had taken refuge on the roof, where she was fed through a tiny upstairs window. She was watched, and was sometimes joined by, another group of cats who found this behavior strange, but bearing certain obvious culinary rewards.

This same roof, with a tiny window for easy access, had proved to be a giant litter box the first winter I spent in that house. I often kept the window cracked for fresh air, and directly under it sat a straw basket filled with rugs. From this basket to the window, and directly to the roof, was a short and interesting journey. Once the snow came, if one were a cat and didn't mind getting slightly cold paws, one could take a nice kitty dump and, lo and behold, it would disappear right into the nice white snow. Imagine my surprise, however—and theirs—when in the spring the snow melted. I was forced to take a shovel to the roof. Next winter I kept this exit to the giant potty in the sky closed.

Beasty stayed on the roof, visible and taking nourishment, for several days as we packed. The day the truck made its appearance for the big pieces, she disappeared and did not make a reappearance until well over a week and a half later, when she fell from the chimney into the empty fireplace directly in front of the very startled new tenant. She was brought to the new house stunned, hungry, and with the small beginning of an unnatural attachment to me that has grown over the years to proportions I find at times overwhelming. She desires never to be separate from me, and when she discovers I have managed to escape, lets forth with a low, continuous howl. At night she curls into a tiny black ball directly by my nose. We share the same pillow. I strongly suspect she feels we also share the same blood. She hates everyone. I, alone among cats and people, am exempt.

She has a twin sister, appropriately called Beauty, a rounder, more elegant version of Beasty. They are deep black and soft to touch, and on both their throats are three perfect white hairs. Beauty is a kitchen cat and spends a great deal of time in a basket on top of the refrigerator. If someone dares beat her to this favorite spot, which she considers exclusively hers, she sits and stares at them until they vacate. She maintains a hypnotic stare and her body seems to tip ever so slightly forward. Remarkably, even if the occupant is asleep, she wakes them with this routine. Could it be she was a queen in another life, and this technique was used for banishment to some far island? A power now limited to removal from favorite baskets.

At one time we thought we had found a kind of minor solution to the major problem of sharing meals with cats: a gift of two rather elaborate water guns—one in the shape of a lion, the other an elephant who shot water through his trunk—kept most cats at a distance during a meal. Certainly it kept one busy and dexterous. Mother and I put these plastic beasts beside our plates and used them frequently and fiercely until the very sight of them in our hands, fingers poised on the triggers, would cause a backing up and a blinking action. However, there was one favorite obese cat, Pumpkin, to whom it posed no threat at all. She would come forward, unblinking, drenched and dripping, like a Sherman tank in a rainstorm, heading for the demolition of the dinner plates.

This water pistol interlude was brought to an abrupt halt one summer evening after we had gone to bed. Lady managed to get both water guns out of the dish drainer. She ate the lion and the elephant. I assume, but do not know for sure, that some sort of celebration took place among the cats who witnessed this plastic massacre. We did not replace the water guns, but reverted to our old, useless, protective gestures, and finally to vegetables. Even then all was not safe, as there seemed to be a growing number of vegetarian and pasta groupies among the carnivores.

Days of Promise

The first memory I have of my father is on a bright summer day. I am very small and I stand looking up into the sky. I can see masses of leaves, first green, then yellow as the warm wind sends them swaying. My father is standing on a truck, the bread truck he drove for Debus Baking Company. He is putting a baby bird back into a nest high, so high, it seems to me he is reaching into the sky.

My mother stands on the wooden stairs leading down from the back porch. The same wooden stairs I sat on when, with great pleasure, I stuck my brother's loose beebees up my nose. It had been a solitary and pleasingly tactile way of spending a soft summer afternoon, sticking those round cool tiny beebees into my baby nose. The discovery of the missing beebees, and the subsequent discovery that they had found themselves up my nose, caused unusual behavior in my mother. A desperate attempt was made to find out just how well I could count so the number of miss-

ing beebees could be determined. My brother was bathed in tears, fearing, yet hoping, for my immediate death. I was not to cry lest the beebees be dislodged in the wrong direction. One nostril was held and I was commanded to blow. Beebees spilled out. Nothing of interest was produced from the other nostril. The doctor was called. It was gently suggested that any remaining beebees might find their way out some other opening. We returned to a kind of mid-afternoon calm.

The day my father returned the bird to its nest, my mother stood looking up, her hand held to her forehead to keep out the sun. A simple familiar gesture, old as time. I have seen it repeated over and over throughout my life. But that was a glittering day. My dark father standing on top of the Debus Baking truck, reaching for a nest, and my mother, with her hand to her forehead, her cotton housedress blowing around the soft parts of her body. A day of glory and promise.

This memory comes from that small midwestern town where I was born, from the first house I recall clearly. One summer afternoon someone brought a coconut into that house. I stood motionless staring at the strange, irregular, hairy brown shell. Tears were stinging my eyelids as the hammer covered with a cloth beat open the shell, and I was assailed with the sight of jagged whiteness. It was my first awareness of insides bursting open. I drank the thin milk and ate the crunchy white. I gazed out the kitchen window and I was intensely happy.

Not far from that house was the big, brick hospital where I was born. My Aunt Adrienne, whom I loved, whom I love even now more than I can put into words, died in her sleep at the beginning of a new year in a tiny house blocks from that hospital. A year later, in the same tiny perfectly kept house, my Uncle George took a gun out of a cigar box, lay down on his bed, his head on a pillow, put the gun in his mouth, and pulled the trigger. My Uncle George, who had sent to me from Florida (where he was stationed before going overseas) a perfect replica of an orange, pocked and beautiful, that opened as if it had been sliced. Inside were twelve tiny bottles of scent with black tops, each fitted into its individual porcelain opening. How I loved that glorious trashy object. It had come close on the heels of a large scarf made from a parachute, tie-dyed deep brown with great bursts of orange and yellow. So soft. I would hold it and jump off the bed, believing in the Movietone image of a soft billowing parachute.

A few minutes in the opposite direction from the hospital was my father's father's house. My grandfather and grandmother lived in that house. I could walk to it from my Aunt Adrienne's. My grandmother died slowly, and six weeks later my grandfather married his mistress, a nice lady from Broken Bow, Nebraska. Family gossip placed her in his arms for the previous twenty-five years. I don't know if this is true. He was a traveling salesman for a flour and feed company. Opportunity must have beckoned from many a small town. But I will never know how they met or how much they loved each other, or if they did. I attended the wedding in Broken Bow, standing in Cuban heels, my hose wrinkling around my ankles.

I liked the new wife who pushed her chair away from the long established Sunday afternoon meal and said: Let's go to the movies. Dishes were abandoned, scraps of food adhering to them. Two o'clock matinee creeping up, let's go to the movies. I respected this. It certainly beat the clearing and washing and scalding and perfect replacing in cupboards that had been my grandmother's unchangeable routine.

Months after bringing home his new bride, my grandfather died of a heart attack in the middle of the night. I was thirteen. I never saw the inside of that house again, but I can close my eyes and remember every piece of furniture, every picture on the wall, the felt-lined drawer in the bedroom where the marbles for the Chinese checkers set were kept in a wooden Old Spice box with a picture of a sailing ship on the lid. I wonder now: Whose Christmas present had that been? Soap on a string nestling in shredded paper, with a bottle of aftershave at the side. The familiar smell still lingered in the soft wooden box you could dent with your nail.

For many years the house was rented, until Aunt Lemo and Uncle Ced retired and moved in. I was gone by then to New York to be an actress. But some days I'm back there, in my grandmother's house, sitting on the cut-plush maroon sofa with carved wooden arms, or falling asleep in the big front bedroom on freshly ironed sheets that Mrs. McDaniel had pressed on the foldout ironing board that fell from the long cabinet in the kitchen. All through these nights I hear the chiming of the clock that sits on the radio cabinet outside the open French doors of that big front bedroom. When there is a lot of company, when the whole family is there—my Uncle Ben and his wife, Mildred, and my only cousin, Patsy, and my mother and father, myself, and my brother—I sleep in a narrow iron bed in the cool basement.

In this same basement, my mother and father sleep in a big bed. One night my father is drunk, and he pees into the drain in the basement floor, the same one I watch the washing machine drain into on Mondays, the sudsy water swirling. I pretend to be asleep, but I hear the whispering, and the great strong sound of my father urinating into the drain. The next day I do the same. I pull down my pants and squat, peeing into the drain. It is the beginning, the first feeling of something sexual, fluttering, secret, hidden.

In this house there is a back bedroom, and from the bed of this room I can see the backyard: the garden, the plum tree, the chicken house, and the garage. I do not remember ever sleeping in this room, but I dream of it often and always there is a curtain instead of a door. A curtain of patterned material that stretches across the door on a wooden rod. I lie in the bed in my dream and watch the sheer window curtains blow in and then out, sticking to the screen. I focus on the minute squares of the screen, and through these squares the lawn appears unnaturally green and thick. My eyes look down at the sidewalk leading from the garage to the back door, one concrete block following another. The cracks seem of immense importance. I turn and watch the curtain falling from the rod where the door should be. I am happy in this dream. It comes before I have collected pain or hurt. It exists only in images of intense pleasure and color.

It was at this house, before I started school, that I experienced my first remembered moment of ecstasy. There were two large trees in the small front lawn. I was running between them, touching one and then the other, feeling for one split second the rough running rivers of bark under my hands. Suddenly between the two trees I was grabbed, I was flung, I was hurled into ecstasy. I looked up through the leaves, and stars fell into my lungs, never to be expelled. I touched the unexplored. Maybe I was only a dizzy child out of breath. I think not. I think something split open and I slipped through the crack. Only part of me came back.

When Colors Ache

Today, on this late afternoon of the first full recognizable day of spring, I walk through the destruction of these woods for the first time. The dogs join me, and secretly behind them Gabby comes, a large grey-blue cat found in a parking lot some ten years ago, then a small kitten with ears like a deer. Following him is Willis, my mother's favorite orange boy, a long lanky troublemaker. Willis and Gabby are sometimes enemies. Today, however, old grievances are put aside as adventure seems forthcoming.

The machines have stopped, left abandoned for the day. It is quiet now except for the sounds we make, the five of us on a walk. We climb, one by one, over what was not long ago the stone fence, and walk toward the marshy land. The trees are gone here, and there are deep ditches made by the massive tires of the machines. Pools of water, like tiny lakes, have filled the ditches. Lady does not hesitate, but leaps into the mud and water with such pleasure, holding tight to one of the many green tennis balls that govern her life, and mine, and anyone who visits. Billy, my older, sedate golden retriever, picks her way about like a child with a new pair of white shoes caught in a rainstorm. She sinks down into the mud with excess weight; extricating herself with a pained expression, she goes to stand on the stone fence. She will wait for us there.

These are not my woods. I never thought of them as mine. They were just part of where I lived. Now thirty-two houses are going to be built. I understand, but something has shifted. Perhaps it is my heart. Why do I cry now? Surely I should have done it on much more important occasions, when I had an audience, a human audience, rather than this group of four animals who, after all, find my sadness boring and inexplicable. There are those in my life who would have rejoiced at seeing me reduced to this hot, tearful vision, and would have counted it a victory. I carry no explanation of this immense hugging sadness, or where I have kept it hidden for so long. It is the end of something. The end of my life here and I am, I admit, frightened. So many years have hung suspended. I have been in flight against the future, and while I was running, it appeared. I am in danger. I recognize the smell.

We walk back to the house, everyone in my footsteps; single file behind me now the animals come. They are subdued by my tears. I see the lights in the house. It is that time of evening, not light and not dark, twilight, if that is the word to encompass this unending changing time, this time when colors ache.

During the summers when I was little and there was no way to be cool, in the evenings after dinner we would get into the car and drive to neighborhoods where other people lived. It was never quite dark, those summer evenings so long ago, when the greens were that particular green color seen only before night made them black, and we would drive through time, through tree-lined streets, and I would see lights. I would see windows and colors. I glimpsed a kind of unfamiliar future. I still look through windows and imagine and remember—not someone else's life, but mine—tables, flowers, curtains, the arm of a chair, a picture, a mirror, books piled on a sill. They all become part of my past and future. Accumulations of glimpses begun in those days driving through green leaves.

When the dark came on us and cool air filled the car, we would drive to A&W and have root beer in frosted mugs, served on trays hooked to the car, and sometimes we would sing, "Mares eat oats and does eat oats and little lambs eat ivy," and I was happy. And the sky was bigger than any sky I have ever seen since.

I see colors now through the windows of the house I live in—rows of books, a piece of soft peach pottery given to me in New Mexico by a gentle man who was my friend. It has a bleached bit of bone tied to its mouth, which was much admired and eventually partly eaten by Billy when she was a young puppy. I can see it now, sitting on a pine chest. Memory saves us sometimes; I use it when I need it, and destroy it when I have to. I will surface. I must. I can't hug pain forever. I will go in and we will eat dinner—these many cats, two dogs, my mother, and myself— and peace will settle, for I have made some kind of peace. Not permanent peace, just the occasional kind.

Once, years ago when I was young, I did a play. The set was a midwestern house in the 1920s, with stained glass around the front door— blues, yellows, reds, and a deep purplish color. A huge lamp hung over a round, wooden table in the living room of this house. There was a rocking chair and a familiar man's chair. To the back, at the center of the stage, were sliding doors that opened to a parlor with a player piano. Everything seemed patterned, dense, and full of touchable color. There was a staircase I believed in, even though it ended in a wooden platform where we stood to wait for our entrances. When the curtain went up and lights came on, the train of fake leaves hanging behind the stained glass of the door would begin to move, gently blown by a hidden fan. I would stand on the stage, watching the scratching of leaves on the glass creating shadows I had seen as a child, in those long days that never ended, in a time that exists only in memory, and I would be transfixed, transported into a space we have no name for. Then in the split of a second I would recover, come hurtling back into reality.

For over a year I lived on that set. I made friends. I met a man and fell in love and stayed in love for many years, and I still love in an old way. Then one night the play ended. I had no way of knowing I would come back to this same stage two more times to play a role. In all, three years of my life spent in this theater on 45th Street, where at nineteen I had stood in the back of the audience and watched an actress who took my breath away. That night I watched something I had dreamed of, but wasn't quite sure existed.

The last time I left this theater, that lady was my friend. After the final performance, I packed up and walked out onto the street in twenty minutes.

In sharp contrast, when the run of the first play ended, I dragged out a year's accumulation of things that took hours to pack up. As the last of my things came down the stairs, a great loading door was pushed open, and I saw an almost empty stage. The house had been seized apart. I had not known, had not prepared for the loss, and I cried, as I cry now for the disappearance of the trees where I live.

Bed. Finally, this beautiful bed. Cats are beginning to stay out at night now. There must be things to do. I wonder what. I leave the door cracked, even though it's still cold, so they can come and go. Everything is quiet except my heart.

The House I Never Left

When I was four, we moved. It was summer and bits of cotton floated in the air. My world changed in one day. We drove away from the town where I was born. Where two sets of grandparents still lived. Where I had learned to walk and talk, to see and to feel.

Here I had started dance class. For weeks I held tight to a bar, staring unflinchingly at the perfect reflection of myself. Surrounded by mirrors, I continued to gaze without distraction at my images. Preparations were advancing for a recital. I was to appear in tap shoes dressed as part of the American flag. Which part was never revealed.

Millions of myself seemed to float in unearthly beauty as I held to the bar. I had never witnessed such perfection, and in such numbers. My romance with my newly discovered self was short-lived. A suggestion was made that I be removed from dance class until I was more mature. I believe that was the phrase that floated above my head the day of my shadowy exit from Flavia Waters's Dance Class for Infants. I was never to be part of the American flag. Occasionally when the afternoons stretched out in the deep summer of that year, I would get out my tap shoes, tie the grosgrain ribbons, and tap up and down the front sidewalk. Dreams die hard.

We moved in the middle of a golden summer. I left my best friend, and we drove the forty miles to our new house. My father would live with his parents during the week, close to the bakery where he worked. His route on the delivery truck started in the early morning. Once, in what seemed to be the middle of the night, I was awakened in the black darkness, lifted up half-asleep into the high front seat of the truck and taken to watch the freshly baked sweet rolls come out on conveyor belts.

Now my father was only home weekends. So began a time without him, which lengthened into the war, when he seemed to disappear altogether. He was to reappear one day without warning, his temper pulled short, sleep filled with nightmares and attacks of malaria. He seemed inordinately angry when I used the Underwood without paper. Ruined ribbon seemed to be uppermost in his mind. My mother had paid no attention at all to the mysterious covered machine and had seemed totally unaffected by my daily typing, with or without paper.

We drove that summer moving day past the one block of buildings that made up the main street of the new town, turned the corner, and drove the three blocks to the house we were to live in. I have never left that house. Never left the heavy summer, watching the heat lifting in waves from the road, sitting in Margretha's garden eating tomatoes bursting with sun, hot to touch, a plate of salt nestled between us, small enough then to feel hidden in rows of green plants.

There were three houses on our new street. An elaborate house stood on one large corner lot—elaborate, that is, to my very young eyes. The foundation and front porch of this house were made of soft, rounded rocks, something I had never before seen, growing up in the wooden and brick Midwest. Years later, the first glimpse of shingled houses in Maine with rounded rock bottoms brought a sharp sting of tears to my eyes.

There was a large, majestic tree that stood on the front lawn. I was told that someone standing under this tree to shelter from a storm was struck by lightning and killed. I have no idea if there was any truth in this story, but I believed with every bit of myself. There wasn't a time when, in the middle of a storm, the possibility of a reoccurrence didn't thrill my childish, bloodthirsty imagination.

Lulu Tomley and her second husband, Sarge, lived in this magical house. Sarge was in a wheelchair. He had married Lulu, his brother's widow. At the time, he'd had the use of his legs. Something had happened; I don't know what. I often thought of him sitting under the great tree on the lawn, in the middle of a storm, when he was struck by lightning and crippled for life. Perhaps he was, after all, the person who was supposed to have died. I was too afraid to ever ask.

I was allowed to visit. I would enter the cool living room. A fireplace of the same round stone seemed to cover one wall. The room was dotted with standing reading lamps. Sarge would move from one to the other with his book as the day progressed. I would settle with a stack of *National Geographic*s, looking at pictures I still dream of.

We would sit after dinner as the darkness started to fall. The pools of light from the lamps became yellower. The wind would change and the curtains start to drift inward, and then, moments from real darkness, I would hear my name called, softly muted by the distance across the empty lot that separated the Tomleys' house and ours. I would start to stack the *National Geographics* back on the shelves that bordered each side of the fireplace. I would linger in that house, waiting for the second call as it floated in the air. When the third call came, it usually included my full name. I became Sandra Dale Dennis. Sandy was gone.

I would walk in almost darkness, past the empty lot and the tall row of cottonwood trees that bordered our house, those silver-grey trees of my plains childhood, whose leaves changed colors as they blew in the wind and drifted bits of silky cotton on the summer air. I would walk up the stairs and onto the porch. Through the screen door, I could see my mother and brother in the light. I was home.

I know now how very small this house was, a miniature of all the houses I came to know. I lived in a world of front porches, with grey-painted wooden floors and sky blue ceilings. A swing hung from chains. Summers were spent on these porches. This particular one was tiny, but in those days, after supper, when the dishes were done and put away in cupboards whose corners were splashed with decals, when the sky darkened to a golden blue and the first cool breeze of the day blew across my forehead, I would lean against my mother. The swing moved gently, on creaking chains, creating air. I would fall asleep with the sound of cicadas clicking in the night, and sometimes the soft drone of grown-up voices.

In those days it was the largest porch in the world. When fall came, leaves would gather in its corners. I would put on a sweater and sit in the late, still, sunny afternoons that smelled of marigolds. As the seasons changed, I would watch from the small living room window as the silver rain fell, packing the leaves into the ground.

When the first snows came, soft fat flakes against a grey sky, I would watch as drifts piled on the wide cement railings. I would escape, dressed like an Eskimo, my scarf tied around the bottom of my mouth. I would dust the snow from the cement railings, shake the drifted swing, make galosh-sized prints down the wooden stairs, the first one out in this perfect untouched white land. My mittened hand trailed the familiar S-curved railings that paraded from the porch, to end with the steps at brick pedestals about two feet from the ground. Years of weather had made the cement as soft as a piece of silk.

In the summers the cement would be hot to the touch. Sometimes we would take the hose and let the water soak into the cement until it cooled and changed color. Streaks of white and grey and specks of black would appear, and then, best of all, that strange glitter, like bits of broken mother-of-pearl. We sat on damp cool cement and sucked on Kool-Aid ice cubes. How long the summers were then. Everything was heavy and ripe with a kind of undefined promise.

Saint-Malo

*M*ay 1974. I am over and over again surprised and overwhelmed with the memory of Saint-Malo. Why does it stick in my head so? That small hotel where Gerry and I seemed to be the only guests. The dining room. We sat at a tiny table next to a radiator for warmth. Evenings and mornings were damp and cold. A young girl with long brown hair waited on us. She was thin and shy but never stopped smiling. She would blush if we ever addressed her directly with any kind of personal remark.

Our room had a heavily patterned wallpaper. A small room, clean and soft. The bed seemed to take up the entire room. Two bedside tables, an armoire, and a chest with tassels attached to the drawer pulls lined the walls. A long window looked directly out on the front lawn. Gold, orange, red fall flowers—those stiff, charged bright flowers that grow late into fall, defying everything. A fish pond of tiny rounded stones filled the lawn. A basin here, and then another, drained, now filled with leaves. Castlelike edifices jumped from these basins lovingly covered with multisized stones. Someone had worked hard and with pleasure to accomplish this strange fairy series of ponds. A cat, whose name was Puss, hid in and around the pond. He perched in early morning mist, noble and foolish. The hotel must have existed as a house in the beginning of its life. Tall and elegant, surrounded by an iron fence, with the sea only a half mile away. Was it because of the sea, or perhaps the time of year, that my mind dwells? Autumn colors pronounced, but grey. Soft, covered with a kind of caul. A cover to be slipped away.

It had not been all bad, she thought as she stood looking out the tall window into the autumn darkness. It was raining and drops hung, slid, and met one another, zigzagging down the window like grey pearls. She could see nothing, but knew what lay outside the window, for she had seen the view from this room earlier in the day. A fierce desire to be alone for a moment, free from him, had taken her back upstairs for a shawl. So she stood for a time, her head leaning against the cool rain-soaked window.

It had not been all bad, this long trip together. Days ago he had stopped working, and they had set off by car and ended up in this tiny hotel somewhere near Saint-Malo. The rages were over for the moment, and he had been gentle and concerned, but always the vision of what had been and what could be lay in her skin. It was not fear, but despair. This was a familiar lull. One that had occurred many times before, in different countries, different rooms, and different beds.

A wet leaf blew onto the window, clung, tracing its way down slowly through trails of rain. The great framed windows in Stockholm had been double, first one and then another, a mirror to the outside. Stockholm remained blue-grey in her memory. The water had combined with the sky, at moments separating into matching but delineated colors, and always this blue steel grey. The Venice of the north, she had read somewhere. There had been a particular violence in Stockholm. Not a physical violence; that or the possibility of that had never occurred. It was a violence of the spirit and a kind violence she was unfamiliar with. Only years later, in that long secret middle life, did she understand. She understood because it became familiar. Because she understood her part in it, and the responsibility shifted.

In Stockholm the couple in the next room had made love continually, it seemed. She heard them late into the night as she lay in bed waiting for him to return from work. Later she woke up to the rushing sound of water and found him asleep, still drunk, peeing a great fountain of water into the air.

In the evenings, when he was gone, she would dress and go down to dinner in the hotel, never feeling quite brave enough to go outside the familiar surroundings. There in that small gleaming dining room she would sit watching, no longer obligated to conversation, scorn, or love. Simply free for a short time. Small golden circles lay like painted suns on the white cloths, reflections from lamps with dusky yellow pleated shades.

Nightly three children would come down to dinner alone. She judged the oldest, a girl, to be about fourteen, the boy perhaps ten, and the littlest girl between five and six. They would order in a very serious way, like adults, without humor. Great pains were taken with the selection but with no accompanying, expected childlike time-consuming indulgences. She would watch them through this ritual. The ordering once accomplished, the facade would break and children would pour forth, only to be buried at the return of any waiter serving or removing food. The signing of the bill was handled with great seriousness. One night the oldest girl ordered a half-bottle of white wine. Glasses were brought. The bottle was shown around the table for inspection and uncorked. A tiny sip was given to the oldest girl who nodded her head and glasses were filled. That night it rained and in the morning the streets were filled with leaves.

In Saint-Malo, she watched as the veined yellow leaf mixed and slid with the milky rain. She turned to pick up the shawl her best friend had sent from a trip to Yugoslavia and, as she turned, the smell of him filled her nostrils. The smell of skin, of warmth enclosed, of dressing and fresh clothes. Something filled her chest and rose to her throat. In the tiny bathroom built into the eaves she settled on her knees in front of the toilet. She settled her body, now dripping with wet. The feeling rose past her throat and spilled.

Moments later she walked down the narrow carpeted staircase to where he was waiting. Dark hair curled around his head. A face full of planes. A fragile, intelligent, dangerous face. She had known even before they arrived at the small hotel somewhere near Saint-Malo, had known the end was inevitable. What she did not know was the number of years it would take to make that final escape.

The Laura Ashley Lady

Six-thirty in the morning and I walk out to this tiny front garden I have started. I like this kind of grey suspended morning. It will be, I think, a soft washed-out day. The machines are silent in the woods. I have half an hour before the sounds begin. How clear in this quiet, the birds. I can smell the earth and I smell green.

Lady follows me and jumps deeply into the newly planted herb garden. Two rows of delicate cilantro and basil flatten and scatter. The strong smell of cilantro fills the air. I do not bother to scold as this bit of earth, this circle at the front door, was only grass when she came here two years ago from New Mexico. She has torn across it too many times to be stopped now by the tag-end tulips, new tiny herbs, and the heavy rocks my niece, Pam, so gently and painstakingly carried from the jumble that used to be a stone fence in the woods. A ringed circle with fanning triangles leads to a tiny middle circle filled with late lilies. This morning it reminds me of some ancient burial ground.

I remember one clear sunny morning on a fall day in Denmark I took a path, a tiny dirt path down to what the signs said were the remains of a burial boat. I wonder now, is this possible? Are there burial boats? What did the signs say? I was alone that day I went inside the earth. A string of unshaded bulbs hung like old torches, casting light in shadows. I saw ribs of wood. Ribs of wood like a giant skeleton. Human ribs. Animal ribs. Everything seemed so symmetrical, so carefully placed. It seems now it had to be part of a plan. In my mind, no kind of anguish had placed these bones. There was something familiar that morning. Something tugged at my insides. What did I recognize? It was not fear. I was not afraid, only alert. The black dampness filled my nostrils. I turned and walked out from under the earth, into the sunlight filled with red tiled roofs and fall leaves. Over twenty years have passed, and this morning I can smell the same earth, close my eyes and see the string of lights and tenderly placed rounded ribs.

When I was little, living in the small midwestern town where I was born, there was a natural history museum and in that museum there was a room with Indian remains. On the left as you entered was a bone pit. Endless and deep it seemed to me as a child. Surrounding it were the rounded iron bars one finds in a playground. I would stand for hours, clinging to the iron fence, peering into this pit, lost in a pile of bones, fragments of human remains lit by colored lights. I remember in particular a kind of phosphorescent green light that played over the bones like water.

This same room contained a large glass case, and in this case was an Indian woman and her baby, mummified. Yellow-brown skin stretched across her face and hands, parchment of human skin. Bits of clothing still clung around her and the wrapped baby. I never wearied of this room, never wearied of the bits of beads and bones and cloth. The colors of the dead.

Years later, in a tiny one-room museum somewhere in England, I laid eyes on a gently placed, carefully labeled specimen of petrified dog feces. A shaft of light pierced the glass case filled with artifacts. Something assailed me, some ghost of the past. Bent over the case, gazing at a marbleized dog turd, I became hysterical with unexplored laughter. I removed myself from the eyes of the uncondemning but mystified English lady who stood like a character out of an Elizabethan novel, longing for something more, or something less.

My feet are soaked. This early morning is damp. Several cats have joined me, picking their way through the wet grass to sit in the garden. How some animals love the possibility of human company. Standing here this early morning in my aqua tennis shoes, extra-large green sweatpants, and ragged T-shirt, I sense a Laura Ashley lady trailing a large picture hat through the dew; a Jane Seymour castle-bound, English-skinned actress, tall and lithe, a basket over my arm for gathering fragrant mulitcolored flowers that I will lovingly arrange to overflowing in vases on polished tables.

Petals will drift to the shiny surfaces and lie gently, pale and curling, like a glimpsed picture in *House and Garden* magazine. Perhaps in this vision I will be photographed stretched languidly on a great down blue-and-white patterned sofa, books and flowers on display, maybe one golden retriever at my feet and a matching orange cat.

This morning, however, I pick seven rather nice petunias. A soft flower, the petunia, but strong. The more you pluck away, the more she repeats herself. These blooms are bluish purple and ruffled. I pick the last of the tulips, ragged edged, bright yellow and red, the end now, the end of the bulbs, except for the lilies which stand tall in the center of the garden like miniature palm trees with extra fronds. When will they bloom? I wonder.

I stupidly dug the garden down. I see now. I should have piled the soil up so I would have had a mound as opposed to a hole. It appears more like a pond filled with dirt than a flower bed. Perhaps in the fall I will add earth when everything has died down. But then will my bulbs come up, or will they be under too much earth? It could be that my fortune will have changed radically, and I will employ a gardener who has never run at the sight of a slug, or marveled at the overnight disap-

pearance of the lacy dill. The vision of green, bereft stems will not cause anguish, wonderment, or openmouthed bewilderment. Such things will not happen under this mythical gardener. My house will be filled with flowers, roses full-blown. Nothing, no one, will eat these soft fragrant petals and leaves. My table will be laden with vegetables and herbs. Friends will come, and we will toss salads and hang herbs to dry, and always the gardener, like the reserved yet feeling butler in *Upstairs, Downstairs,* will watch with affection and humor. I close my eyes and dream of things I've seen on PBS.

Of course, if all else fails, this next spring I could just, by myself, dig the hole deeper and fill it with water. I would then have a large mud hole surrounded by rocks. I could acquire a few baby pigs and they could live right outside the front door. This seems a much more realistic dream.

The lilacs are so full this year and, for the first time since I have lived here, a bush that never bloomed produced all sorts of floppy pale-purple flowers. In the morning when I wake there is a window directly in front of my eyes, one not very large window, with bright yellow curtains, and through the opening of these curtains I can see the top of the lilac bush. It fills the few inches of space with tall, full purple blossoms and on grey days the colors take on a deep shade, for nothing reflects or disturbs and all seems caught in water.

The machines have started, trucks and wood chewers. The steady noise will continue through the day until late afternoon. How unaccustomed I have been to any but the familiar sounds of my own life—the animals, the dishwasher whishing, rain and sleet against the windows, the sound of a car coming up the driveway, in the winter the shifting of the furnace turning on and off—and now this spring, a continual roar, an invasion approaching.

I walk round the house to the back. This has always been my favorite, this flat English lawn falling straight to the woods. Not one tree, only this lovely long lawn. Bushes have nearly taken over the small back garden, poison oak for certain, and great lush tangles of unrecognizable plants—a cats' jungle, this low heavy thicket of green things. Such a place to play. Cool, too, I suppose. In other years we have kept the garden clear and filled: rows of tomatoes, zucchini, failed brussels sprouts that attained only a tiny pea-sized growth. Beautiful tall plants marching with miniature brussels sprouts. Little perfect replicas of brussels sprouts. I waited these out until they froze.

One year we grew pumpkins of unnatural strength and size. They grew and grew until everything seemed filled with varying shades of orange. And there was the year Eric planted sunflowers. They reached to great heights, reminding me of something gone wrong. They lifted themselves like monster umbrellas, and sometime in the late autumn thousands of tiny grey seeds started to fall. Then came the slaughter of the birds. Stupid, stupid, I thought as I waved my arms day after day, screaming obscenities at cats who watched me with unblinking contempt. The house seemed to fill with the dead and the half-dead, flapping wings and hooded eyes.

Then I Will Remember

Yesterday I buried a cat in the little back garden filled now with only the curling brown leaves of tulips and daffodils. Nothing blooming and weeds starting to take hold. I found him on the road early in the morning as I went for groceries. Big he was, it seemed from the car. He must have been hit and thrown to the curb, or maybe he had almost made it across when the blow came. I stopped and picked him up, still and unyielding. His eyeball was separated from the socket, hanging by strange threads. His jaw smashed. Beautiful big black-and-white stray. Big, thin, muscular unaltered male. How long on his own? I muse. How many times had he crossed this street? Thin long ears pocked with battle nicks. I wonder could I have caught him or would he have escaped me? I doubt he held much trust in people. Nothing to do now but bury him in the backyard. He rides home with me on the front seat, lengthy and stiff. The dogs who have gone shopping with me find this cat interesting but unusually quiet. At home I wrap him in an old towel and put him in the shed to wait till the day cools down. Then I will dig a hole.

I go into the kitchen to wash my hands and drink a glass of cold water and am surrounded by life. Cats on counters. Dogs stretched on the cool floor. I stand at the sink looking out the window, glass in my hand, time suspended, as I try to think who has been buried in this backyard. Little Boy is here, I know, for I buried him myself one summer afternoon. Late that same evening I went out to grieve and fell over a large standing pipe in the yard. Gashed my shin and sprawled headfirst into the dirt. I stopped my mourning and turned full attention on myself. Bobbie and Octavia are here too. Those I remember. There are more. Time has made me forget. Eric's kittens are here. Six of them, one after the other they died, as their mother seemed to grow stronger and more pleased with each tiny death. A witch of a white cat. Here somewhere near the clothesline pole is Little Girl, that gentle sister of Little Boy.

In the late afternoon we dig a hole, my brother and I. My brother who is kind of a stranger to me. I think we have not seen each other for ten years. A big blond man with glasses. A face that reminds me of my mother. I place the towel-wrapped cat in the long soft damp hole. We cover him with earth and pile stones on the grave. In time I will forget the summer heat, the slight but certain smell coming from the towel. I will forget that my brother and his tall wife came for a visit. I will forget until that moment next summer, or summers from now, when the light filters through the leaves, lacing the grass, when there is that faint cooling breeze so familiar and calming on a hot day. When I wonder about death—mine, and the animals that surround me—then I will remember. I will catch a glimpse of something.

From These Windows

$\mathcal{I}$'m writing. Months have gone by since I stopped making any real attempt to continue what I had told everyone I had started. Bits and pieces scribbled on familiar yellow pads float around, reminding. So today, this beautiful Indian summer day, this fake October day when the temperature rises to the seventies, I gather up the bits and pieces, including my abandoned writing board now defaced on two ends by cats who have used it for a scratching post, and I sit at my table and look out this window and I'm lost.

What changes have taken place outside this window and how aware I suddenly am of the days that have passed since I came home. The visions from these windows are stored, stacked, stabbed into my eyes. Why didn't I write them down at the time? I think it is because I am grotesquely secret. Not for any selfish enfolding reason. Perhaps whatever gave me green eyes and tiny nails on my little fingers gave me this secret nature. My mother, when questioned by me about myself as a child, said something to the effect that when I was handed to her as a new baby, I pulled two window shades down over my eyes. This amuses me, and still continues to drive her to distraction. Was I born with this nature, or was it that I recognized at that moment the enormous mistake I had made? She counts it important enough to speak about. She must have guessed something, and I have kept the same dismissal for fifty-two years. Somewhere behind those closed lids visions appeared.

Today I see the fall. Deep purple, reds, and yellows. I see nasturtiums still blooming, their leaves like miniature lily pads. The bed of fresh-dug earth where we planted bulbs of all sorts. I wonder does this warmth confuse them? The late-blooming cosmos swing tall and delicate next to the large, round green tomatoes that never ripened.

I really do not question where I will be in the spring. I will be here to see the bulbs that Chan, Luke, and I planted. It is not a question of can I stay alive until then. I think it simply isn't the right time to die of this cancer. I think I will know when to let go, for I do not think I am afraid of dying. I am not sure, of course, until I face the moment, but now there are too many things to do. I'm not finished finishing things. But then I never will be. I shall die trying to get my taxes in order.

Chan is mowing the grass. I smell it. This will be the last mowing till late spring. Soon we will rake the leaves over the flower beds and hope for the best. In the spring I will pick strange-colored tulips to put in the house, and the cats will bite the stems and chew the leaves. This is the way things are.

Tomorrow I am taking a blind kitten. Today, Momma sits on my desk and Teddy on the windowsill looks longingly outdoors. Teddy is

68

new, a large, beautiful orange tabby, soft as silk, who spends an inordinate amount of time humping soft blankets. This feat is accomplished by grabbing the blanket with his teeth, straddling it, and then humping away. This strange but harmless habit is given a certain amount of attention by myself and several cats. A kind of soft-core porno kitty circle has grown up around this almost daily performance. True, we have become slightly blasé, and the first flush of excitement has melted into mild interest. Teddy was given to me by Brenda, who informed me that he had almost died fooling around with a loose-knit blanket. His head had gone through a large opening, and he was found almost strangled. This near brush with death has not dampened his affection for blankets and feats of sexual daring.

I thought to start early this morning. I failed. A cat threw up between the washing machine and the dryer. This tiny place, this sliver of space filled with cat throwup. Why in this large house was the choice made to throw up between the washer and dryer? I think vengeance is the answer. The cleanup was time consuming.

I seem to have read somewhere that most writers write in the morning. It occurred to me that what works for Iris Murdoch might work for me. It also occurs to me she might be more adept at writing than I am. In fact, she could probably write in the evenings too. I could write if I had a pine table in my kitchen and one very amusing cat and if I lived in Oxford.

However, it is now eleven A.M. I have fed the cats, scrubbed the counters, washed out the ice box, spackled the holes in the guest room—not to mention cleaning what happened between the washer and dryer.

I will write now. Later, when the spackle dries, I'm going to paint and I promise myself I will not make a mess. It will be beautiful. White, stark white. A lovely blue-and-white Canadian quilt on the bed. I will finish this weekend and hope it inspires me to do my own rooms.

Just now I straighten my desk and find in a folder some pages I had written in the spring. So I did put down something after all. Why didn't I take advantage of that enforced time I spent in bed? Over a month I lay there, listening to the construction about me. I thought and thought, and drifted with pleasure. I had guests. And then one day I started to move. I went back to teaching. I drove again. Sometimes I was so tired I would sleep for hours in the middle of the day. It seemed to me I could do only little bits of things. I still have only a small amount of the energy

I used to have, but I can do everything slowly. In late November I will have another operation and three more treatments of chemotherapy for ovarian cancer. Funny, those little things can do so much damage. My knowledge of my body is a bit like my knowledge of geography. Surprisingly minimal. I was fairly aware of the position of my heart and brain, but never considered the ovaries. I had not thought with them, or said the pledge of allegiance with my hand over them. Nevertheless, one ovary had a life of its own. I think it foolish for having drawn such attention to itself.

Another Spring

April. It looks a brilliant cool sunny morning. I woke at 4:30 A.M. and watched from deep darkness till now. One can watch darkness, blackness. It is full of things. Now it is 7:00 A.M. and the light seems to be coming from the right, quite high. I am limited, for the time, to this one window next to my bed. The sun hits the tumble of bushes and turns the new green to wet crystals. I have watched these bushes, this tangle of ground growth turn a soft green. Tomorrow, Monday, I will have been home one week, and in that week I have seen the faint lacy green begin in the distance, the woods behind the stone fence, and it has moved closer and fuller. So it seems to have grown as I watched. The trees are still winter-stripped, though driving home last week the willows were a soft yellow-green and the flowering trees almost at bursting point. My lilac has lovely green leaves, but it sits directly in front of the vent for the dryer and may have a sense of false security.

How strange, how very strange it is to be limited to this bed. To hear other people get up. To hear the familiar chores that I did with such pleasure being accomplished by someone else breaks my heart. Silly. Anyone in their right mind would certainly be glad someone else was cleaning kitty litter boxes. But I miss this beginning of the day. I am not unhappy. I am happy and drift in great calmness, but I am angry at my lack of physical ability. Cancer. Unexpected strange disease. Certainly not on my agenda.

The cats, however, find this change in bed habits entirely in their favor. I am surrounded at all times. My pens disappear. Papers are chewed. Flowers brought in from the garden are eaten like something alive in front of my eyes and always, always, there is this great warmth and comfort, these soft gentle sleepy bunches of different natures.

I have never known this kind of enforced bed life. Trays of food are brought up. I have to ask for things. Strangest of all to have to ask. I can get up, but it takes all my energy and resembles a rhinoceros hauling itself out of a mud bath. Great, ungainly flapping movements and grunts accompany this getting out of bed ritual. I want to be what I was, and I have not yet learned to be fond of the great map of scars and holes that march across my stomach. And what is this colostomy business? I mean how on earth can such a diversion take place? But spring is on its way slowly out my window. I recognize the urgency. I smell the beginning.

This morning Jake sits on my papers, a gift of an all-black, six-toed blind cat. Last fall he came, September I think, two months old and blind from birth. I have watched him with such joy. He is everywhere in these two rooms where I spend so much of my time. Nothing has escaped him.

Not even the highest peaks. He climbs up my wooden furniture as if it were a great bark-covered tree. When he has accomplished a height and wants to get down, he puts out a paw in the air, trying to touch another surface so as to gradually make his way down. When he discovers nothing, he finally leaps. Knowing, I suppose, there is always something. There has been for him always the floor, and he knows it well. For him it is filled with security. It is filled as well with bits of paper, pens, multiple games, places to hide.

The bed is his. He climbs the sheets. He knows my bed table well and can hear the sound of my food tray touch the surface. He runs, flinging himself on the table. Bananas and strawberries this morning. He has discovered the toilet and sits for hours on the stool with one paw drooping into the water.

Many cats live in these two rooms. Some are his friends, some enemies. Not bitter enemies, just not friends. Teddy is his best friend, a large orange marmalade. They sleep entwined in a large basket on the table, legs thrown across one another. Teddy is forever patient, though sometimes rough at play. But Jake never backs down. He trusts Teddy.

Jake likes the dogs and snuggles close to them. Their great size seems nothing to him. What I find remarkable is his heightened sense of play and desire to explore. Strangely, nothing frightens him except a new voice or a loud sound. He is totally devoted to the destruction of toilet paper. I've had to hide it in a container.

I love to watch the way he walks. Those great extra-toed front paws, like a clown with large shoes. He makes me laugh. He makes me forget dying.

I think I have no real escape except through this. These few fragile words I can manage every day. I must think, I must let myself explore what I'm feeling and thinking. I need to explore that black territory. I do not want to drift into death if that is now to be. I want to keep track as long as I can. For weeks I have avoided thought, I have avoided pain, and it is a viable way of maintaining life. I have laughed. Cooked. Entertained. Drunk wine. Read without end, stringing one book to another. I have been alone and I have been with my friends and I have been happy, but I am avoiding some large upheaval, some change. Something is meant to happen and I, like an ostrich, have been hiding, and I must stop now. Dying is too easy to avoid. I cannot let it pass unexplored. It is mine. It has been given to me. I am responsible for finding out how I feel. There is a strong possibility I will escape this particular death. In fact, I think I will, but I must know what I'm feeling. I am still strongly bound by my old behavior. That secret child is an even more secret middle-aged woman. I know I shall not break this secrecy. It is a deep part of my nature, but I can create out of this hidden life.

It is one of those first spring mornings I have been longing for. The sun is in patches everywhere. Cats fill the windows. No leaves yet. Just a faint green beginning in the undergrowth. The daffodils are almost done. Soon there will be tulips. Strange unfamiliar tulips like the daffodils. I had quite forgotten what I had planted. Pale yellow with bright orange centers. Bright yellow with dark orange centers. A lovely fluted double daffodil, one layer of the palest yellow with a slightly deeper yellow on top, like something made out of sunshine. And the great, tall large yellow daffies, so strong looking with a great bell in the middle.

And the four tiny tight-budded peonies Bill brought to me over the weekend. That such a display could be hidden inside that pink-green bud. Even the cats are surprised at the floppy, large many-petaled mops and find them extremely hard to munch.

My mind languishes soft. It dwells on images it can see at the moment. This orange room. The long cherry table at my bedside, covered with things I find comforting. Layers of books, a peach platter that holds my medicine and water. A blue-and-white bowl filled with gentle scent and a giant pinecone Luke brought back from California. It is so large and unfamiliar I thought at first someone had made it.

This time seems so powerful. Perhaps it is the luxury of time being here almost helpless. I see without the burden of time past or visions of the future. Piles of dirty clothes in a basket assail my eyes with such color. The bamboo blinds hanging on three windows change with every outside light, throwing patterns of slants on the bookcase. Painted sticks of sunshine and dark. My soft orange glass-shaded lamp slips me so gently into twilight and then darkness. How I love.

Sandy Dennis

Afterword

SANDY DENNIS, born in the spring of 1937, died in the early spring of 1992. She was at home in her bed, as she wanted to be. Two close friends, her dog, and several cats were nearby, including Christian, a dark tabby she estimated to be about twenty-one years old. She referred to him as "the quiet old man."

In the still hours before dawn, Christian slept on the pillow beside her. When Sandy's shallow breathing ceased and she was gone, Christian raised his head, stood up, opened his mouth, and uttered a silent meow.

*L*OUISE LADD has published widely, including seventeen humorous novels for young adults, and is a freelance editor. A graduate of Wellesley College, she has taught at Manhattenville College and leads The Writer's Workshop at Fairfield University. For nineteen years she produced Doug Taylor's Connecticut Center Acting Ensemble, where she also performed in many plays. One of her fondest memories is being directed by Sandy Dennis in a female version of Neil Simon's *The Odd Couple.*

*D*OUG TAYLOR is a playwright, actor, and director. More than thirty-five of his live dramas were aired during the Golden Age of Television, and dozens of his plays have been produced, including *Horse Johnson* on Broadway, starring Jack Klugman and Jill Clayburgh. He has directed more than fifty plays and acted in numerous professional productions. A graduate of the University of California at Berkeley and the Neighborhood Playhouse, he is founder and artistic director of the Connecticut Center Acting Ensemble at Fairfield University, where he trains his acting company. One of the brightest moments in his career was playing opposite Sandy Dennis in *Same Time, Next Year,* where the two took turns directing each other amid great good spirits and much laughter.

More Papier-Mache Press Titles of Related Interest

Full Moon: Reflections on Turning Fifty
Susan Carol Hauser

Full Moon honors, rather than shuns the rich passage of time. These celebratory essays and the accompanying exquisite four-color art represent the thirteen moon cycles in the year leading up to a woman's fiftieth birthday, reflecting on personal aging.

"These graceful meditations...are dotted with wry humor and complemented by the delicate art of California-based Barbara Van Arnam" —Publishers Weekly

ISBN 0-918949-93-9, hardcover

From May Sarton's Well: Writings of May Sarton
Selection and Photographs by Edith Royce Schade

Edith Royce Schade's striking black-and-white photographs accompany May Sarton's renowned prose and poetry, as a piano accompanies a lyric singer—sometimes in unison, often in harmony, occasionally in counterpoint. These photographic reflections illuminate the intimacy and inspiration that come from reading Sarton.

"I can't think of a better introduction to Sarton's writing than this collection....From May Sarton's Well *is a book to be treasured*" —Bay Area Reporter

ISBN 0-918949-51-3, trade paper

ISBN 0-918949-52-1, hardcover

In the Garden of Our Own Making
Barbara Sperber

A bittersweet tale of a lifelong mother-daughter struggle. Years after giving up her daughter for adoption, a woman sits with her dying mother. Experiencing the life-giving cycle of family, love, and loss, she reunites with her own daughter and shapes a new kind of love with the people in her life.

"*Barbara Sperber has given us a secret garden where mothers and daughters grow bitter herbs and passion flowers. She has made poetry out of the dark soil of separation and loss.*" —Betty Jean Lifton, PhD, *author of* Journey of the Adopted Self

ISBN 0-918949-69-6, trade paper

Papier-Mache Press

$\mathcal{A}$t Papier-Mache Press, it is our goal to identify and successfully present important social issues through enduring works of beauty, grace, and strength. Through our work we hope to encourage empathy and respect among diverse communities, creating a bridge of understanding between the mainstream audience and those who might not otherwise be heard.

We appreciate you, our customer, and strive to earn your continued support. We also value the role of the bookseller in achieving our goals. We are especially grateful to the many independent booksellers whose presence ensures a continuing diversity of opinion, information, and literature in our communities. We encourage you to support these bookstores with your patronage.

We publish many fine books about women's experiences. We also produce lovely posters and T-shirts that complement our anthologies. Please ask your local bookstore which Papier-Mache items they carry. To receive our complete catalog, send your request to Papier-Mache Press, 135 Aviation Way, #14, Watsonville, CA 95076, or call our toll-free number, 800-927-5913.